Geoff Tibballs is the author of over 150 books, including the bestselling *Mammoth Book of Jokes, The Mammoth Book of Dirty Jokes, The Mammoth Book of Comic Quotes, The Seniors' Survival Guide* and *Dad-isms*. He has contributed to the *Ripley's Believe It or Not!* annuals for more than twenty years. He lives in Nottingham with his wife.

1001 ONE-LINERS

Geoff Tibballs

First published in the UK in 2023 by Ad Lib Publishers Ltd
15 Church Road
London SW13 9HE
www.adlibpublishers.com

Text © 2023 Geoff Tibballs

Paperback ISBN 9781802471212
eBook ISBN 9781802471922

A CIP catalogue record for this book is available
from the British Library.

Every reasonable effort has been made to trace copyright-holders of
material reproduced in this book, but if any have been inadvertently
overlooked the publishers would be glad to hear from them.

Printed in the UK
10 9 8 7 6 5 4 3 2 1

MIX
Paper | Supporting
responsible forestry
FSC® C171272

INTRODUCTION

Short, quick-fire jokes have been popular for centuries. Indeed, the world's oldest surviving joke book, the *Philogelos*, which was written in Ancient Greek, contains this classic doctor joke:

Patient: "Doctor! When I wake up I'm all dizzy. Then after half an hour I feel fine."
Doctor: "Well, wait half an hour before waking up."

Meanwhile in Rome, they had a gag for every occasion, from senate orations and lavish feasts to throwing Christians to the lions. A Cicero stand-up gig was the hottest ticket in town.

Shakespeare readily slipped one-liners into his comedies, while medieval jesters used pithy quips to amuse the royal court, well aware that if the joke backfired and somehow offended the monarch, their next audience might be with the executioner. "Dying on stage" carried a more sinister meaning for comedians in those days.

It's not hard to see why one-liners remain in vogue with today's comedians. They are easy to remember, quick to deliver and if one gag dies on its feet, the next is waiting in the wings, hopefully to a better reception.

Here I have compiled some of the best one-liners around – a heady mix of old and new favourites, dad jokes, thoughtful musings, corny puns and witty observations, covering a vast range of topics from Families to Fish, Money to Music, Relationships to Religion and from Technology to Travel.

They can be used to brighten up business conferences where the delegates are as tired as the sandwiches; dinner parties where the conversation is threatening to slide into a discussion about spreadsheets; seemingly interminable Zoom calls; and, of course, in speeches at weddings that are so emotional that even the cake is in tiers.

Geoff Tibballs, 2023

ACCIDENTS

I accidentally handed my wife a glue stick instead of a chapstick. She still isn't talking to me.

A truck carrying snooker equipment has crashed on the highway. The driver is under a rest and the cues stretch back for miles.

Kids in the back seat cause accidents; accidents in the back seat cause kids.

Did you hear about the man who was hit on the head with a can of soda? – He was lucky it was a soft drink.

Did you hear about the optometrist who fell into his lens-grinding machine? – He made a spectacle of himself.

Did you hear about the actor who fell through the floor last year? – It was just a stage he was going through.

Two ships collided. One was carrying a cargo of red paint, and the other was carrying blue paint. All the crew and passengers were marooned.

I spilt some stain remover on my shirt. I don't know how I'm going to get it out.

***

ADVICE

Before you judge a man, walk a mile in his shoes. After that who cares? He's a mile away and you've got his shoes! – Billy Connolly

If you're ever attacked by a gang of circus performers, always go for the juggler.

Never underestimate the power of stupid people in large groups.

Never hit a man with glasses. Hit him with something bigger and heavier.

Never trust a dog to watch your food.

Never believe a man who says "trust me" or a woman who says "it's fine".

Be careful: the toes you step on today may be connected to the ass you have to kiss tomorrow.

Accept that some days you're the pigeon and some days you're the statue.

If at first you don't succeed, destroy all evidence that you tried.

A good rule to remember for life is that when it comes to plastic surgery and sushi, never be attracted by a bargain.
– Graham Norton

When all else fails, read the instructions.

Never put a child wearing Superman pyjamas in the top bunk.

Never lie to an X-ray technician. They can see right through you.

Don't hate yourself in the morning – sleep till noon.

Whatever you do, always give 100 per cent – unless you're donating blood.

Ever have trouble opening a bottle of champagne? My advice: hit it with a ship. I've seen people do that. It works. – Russell Kane

Never argue with the person who is packing your parachute.

Never trust a barber with blood on his shirt.

Never go to a doctor whose office plants have died.

When you're arguing with an idiot, try to make sure he isn't doing the same.

Never laugh at your partner's choices – you're one of them.

If you can't be kind, at least have the decency to be vague.

If you can keep your head while others around you are losing theirs, you may want to land your helicopter someplace else.

Treat each day as your last; one day you will be right.

My grandfather likes to give me advice, but he's a little forgetful. One day, he took me aside and left me there. – Steven Wright

***

ALCOHOL

Alcohol is a perfect solvent. It dissolves marriages, families and careers.

I've been on that new whisky diet. I lost three days last week.

Whisky is a great drink. It makes you see double and feel single.

What device tells you that you've drunk too much? – A karaoke machine.

My father drank so heavily, when he blew on the birthday cake he lit the candles. – Les Dawson

Is it okay to start drinking as soon as the kids are at school … or am I a really bad teacher?

Wife: "What's the idea of coming home half drunk?"
Husband: "Sorry. I ran out of money."

I just heard someone shouting: "Tequila! Vodka!
Whisky!" I said: "Hey, I call the shots around here."

I'm the only one in my family who drinks, which is great
because to me they're all potential liver donors.

Did you hear about the guy who poured beer over his
newly seeded lawn in the hope that the grass would
come up half cut?

We call my uncle the exorcist, because every time he
visits he rids the house of spirits.

Many things can be preserved in alcohol. Dignity is not
one of them.

When I read about the evils of drinking, I gave up
reading. – Henny Youngman

You know you're drunk when you get out of bed and
miss the floor.

A drunk wakes up in a police cell and asks the officer: "Why am I here?" "For drinking," says the officer. "Great," says the drunk. "Let's get started."

Abstinence is a good thing, but it should always be practised in moderation.

***

ANIMALS

A friend asked me if I could help him round up 27 cows. I said: "Yes, of course. That's 30 cows."

Why did the hedgehog cross the road? – To see his flat mate.

What do you call a deer with no eyes? – No eye deer.

What do you call a deer with no eyes and no legs? – Still no eye deer.

What do you call a cow with no legs? – Ground beef.

I was watching a dog chasing its tail and thinking: "Dogs are easily amused." Then I realised I was watching a dog chasing its tail.

Why do dogs always run to the door whenever the doorbell rings? It's hardly ever for them.

Dogs are the leaders of the planet. If you see two life forms, one of them's making a poop, the other's carrying it for him, who would you assume is in charge? – Jerry Seinfeld

My dog can count. I know this because I asked him what is two minus two and he said nothing.

A police officer knocked on my door and told me that my dogs were chasing people on bikes. My dogs don't even own bikes.

My new dog goes and sits in a corner every time the doorbell rings. He's a boxer.

I named my dog Five Miles so I can tell people I walk Five Miles every day.

My neighbour's dog is called Blacksmith because every time the front door is opened he makes a bolt for it.

My friend's dog loves to eat garlic. His bark is far worse than his bite.

At what age is it appropriate to tell my dog that he's adopted?

The most affectionate creature in the world is a wet dog. – Ambrose Bierce

I have a dog to provide me with unconditional love, but I also have a cat to remind me that I don't deserve it. It's all about balance.

Dogs have owners; cats have staff.

How did a cat take first prize at the bird show? – By reaching into the cage.

What did the cat do after eating cheese? – He waited by a mouse hole with baited breath.

Why do you always find the cat in the last place you look? – Because you stop looking after you find it.

I've opened a deer cloning service. It's for anyone looking to make a quick buck.

I told my niece that I saw a moose on the way to work this morning. She said: "How do you know he was on his way to work?"

Did you hear about the two silkworms that had a race? – It ended in a tie.

If, as is often claimed, hippos can run and swim faster than humans, then cycling is your only chance of beating a hippo in a triathlon.

How do you know when two octopuses are dating? – They walk arm in arm, in arm, in arm, in arm, in arm, in arm, in arm, in arm.

Why don't lobsters like to share? – Because they're shellfish.

I went to the zoo the other day and an elephant tried to charge me. I told him I'd already paid.

What do you give an elephant with diarrhoea? – Plenty of room.

Why are elephants wrinkled? – Have you ever tried to iron one?

Did you hear about the man who had a job at the zoo circumcising elephants? The wages were poor, but the tips were huge.

Which antelope was the most feared in the African savannah? – Vlad the Impala.

Did you know that dolphins are so smart that within a few weeks of captivity they can train someone to stand on the edge of their pool and throw fish to them?

Hedgehogs. Why can't they just share the hedge? – Dan Antopolski

A family go to the zoo, but the only animal in the entire zoo is a dog. It's a shih tzu.

***

ANXIETY

Worrying works! More than 90 per cent of the things I worry about never happen.

The human body is 80 per cent water. So basically we are just cucumbers with anxiety.

Research shows that getting facial tattoos can eliminate some forms of anxiety. For example, you'll never need to worry about finding a job.

I often worry about my attention span, but not for long.

I'm so stressed, I might go potholing. I tend to cave under pressure.

My doctor is so considerate. He knows I suffer from anxiety so he put both his hands on my shoulders to comfort me during my prostate exam.

***

APPEARANCE

I told my girlfriend she drew her eyebrows too high. She looked surprised.

A recent study has found that women who carry a little extra weight live longer than the men who mention it.

I never forget a face, but in your case I'd be glad to make an exception. – Groucho Marx

I used to hate facial hair, but then it grew on me.

A beard can hide a multitude of chins.

If I had a pound for every woman who found me unattractive, they would eventually find me attractive.

Beauty is only skin deep, but ugly goes all the way to the bone.

Nobody is ugly after 2 am.

Finally my winter fat has gone. Now I have spring rolls.

I married my wife for her looks, but not the ones she's been giving me lately.

You know you're not attractive when it comes to a group photo and they hand you the camera.

"Hello, everyone. Welcome to Cosmetic Surgery Addicts Anonymous. I see a lot of new faces here tonight."

***

ART

I've finally decided to retire after a long career as a graffiti artist. To be honest, the writing's been on the wall for some time.

What did the artist draw before he went to bed? – The curtains.

Two small boys ended up in a modern-art gallery. "Quick!" said one. "Run before they say we did it!"

I failed my art exam because I used the wrong pencil. I guess it wasn't 2B.

Why did Van Gogh become a painter? – Because he didn't have an ear for music.

Why did the artist think he was going to jail? – Because he had been framed.

Did you hear about the boy who had a fight with his art teacher? – He drew blood.

What's the difference between an art student and a philosophy student? – A philosophy student asks you *why* you want fries with that.

***

BABIES

People who say they sleep like a baby usually don't have one.

A woman asked the doctor: "Should I have another baby after 39?" The doctor replied: "No, 39 children is enough."

Watching a baby being born is a little like watching a wet St. Bernard coming in through the cat door. – Jeff Foxworthy

A woman said to the dentist: "I don't know which is worse, having a tooth pulled or having a baby." The dentist replied: "Well, make up your mind. I've got to adjust the chair."

Why do the wives of taxi drivers rarely get pregnant? – Because taxi drivers have a habit of pulling out unexpectedly.

Did you hear about the pregnant bed bug? – She's going to have her baby in the spring.

A woman in labour suddenly started shouting: "Didn't, Wouldn't, Couldn't, Shouldn't!" "Don't worry," said the doctor. "Those are just contractions."

Why did the man bring his pregnant wife a small lizard? – She told him to get a baby monitor.

Anyone who says it's as easy as taking candy from a baby has never tried it.

"No thanks, I'm a vegetarian" is a fun thing to say when someone hands you their baby.

What do you call it when you're giving birth but nobody is there to help? – A midwife crisis.

Why is a pregnant girlfriend like burnt toast? – In both cases the guy thinks: "If only I'd taken it out sooner."

How do we know that passing a kidney stone is worse than giving birth? – Because people often say they want another baby, but no one has ever said they want another kidney stone.

What do you do when your daughter is pregnant but claims she hasn't slept with anyone? – Start a religion.

Did you know, if you get pregnant in the Amazon, it's next-day delivery? – Mark Simmons

A girl broom told a boy broom she was pregnant. "You can't be!" said the boy broom. "We haven't even swept together!"

My mother always believed that labelling children was wrong, which caused chaos in the maternity ward.

***

BARS

A limbo champion walks into a bar ... and is immediately disqualified.

A sandwich walks into a bar. The bartender says: "Sorry, we don't serve food here."

A dung beetle walks into a bar and asks: "Is this stool taken?"

Two jump leads walk into a bar. The bartender says: "I'll serve you, but don't start anything."

Three fonts walk into a bar. The bartender says: "We don't serve your type in here."

A woman walks into a bar and asks for a double entendre. So the barman gave her one.

William Shakespeare walks into a bar. The bartender says: "I can't serve you – you're Bard!"

A man walks into a bar with a roll of tarmac under his arm and says to the bartender: "A pint, please, and one for the road."

Two termites walk into a bar. One asks: "Is the bar tender here?"

The past, the present and the future walk into a bar. It was tense.

An ancient Roman walks into a bar, holds up two fingers and says: "Five beers, please."

Charles Dickens walks into a bar and orders a Martini. The bartender asks: "Olive or twist?"

A skeleton walks into a bar and says to the bartender: "I'll have one beer and a mop."

A cable TV installer walks into a bar. The bartender says: "You'll be served sometime between 7 and 1."

A perfectionist walks into a bar. Apparently the bar wasn't set high enough.

"We don't serve time travellers here," said the bartender. A time traveller walks into a bar.

***

BIRDS

My wife told me to stop impersonating a flamingo. I had to put my foot down.

Why do birds fly south in the winter? – Because it's too far to walk.

You can never lose a homing pigeon. If your homing pigeon doesn't come back, what you've lost is a pigeon.

Why do you never see owls mating when it's raining? – Because it's too wet to woo.

What do you call a chicken crossing the road? – Poultry in motion.

Why did the rubber chicken cross the road? – To stretch her legs.

Why did the chicken cross the road, roll in mud, then cross the road again? – He was a dirty double-crosser.

I bought a bag of bird seed nearly two months ago. Does anyone know how long it takes for the bird to grow?

***

BODY

If your feet smell and your nose runs, you're built upside-down.

What do you call a man with a rubber toe? – Roberto.

If God had meant us to touch our toes, he would have put them further up our body.

What is that tingly sensation you get when you really like someone? – It's common sense leaving your body.

I have a problem with people who are missing body parts. I guess I must be lack-toes intolerant.

What's the least sensitive part of the penis? – The man attached to it.

What's the most sensitive part of a man's body during masturbation? – His ears.

After you die, what part of the human body is the last to stop working? – Your pupils; they dilate.

What's a woman's favourite body part? – I can't remember, but it's on the tip of my tongue.

***

BOOKS

I bought the world's worst thesaurus. Not only is it terrible, it's also terrible.

I'm reading a book about anti-gravity. I can't put it down.

I wrote a book about how to fall down the stairs without hurting yourself. It's a step-by-step guide.

A bit of advice: never read a pop-up book about giraffes.
– Sean Lock

I just wrote a book on reverse psychology. Don't buy it.

I also wrote a book about poltergeists. I'm happy to say it's really been flying off the shelves.

I asked the librarian: "Can you show me where the self-help books are?" She said: "No, that would defeat the object."

Two books meet in a bookstore. One says: "You look so much slimmer than the last time I saw you." "Thanks," said the other. "I had my appendix removed."

What does Charles Dickens keep in his spice rack? – The best of thymes, the worst of thymes.

Three months ago, I logged onto a website and ordered the book *How to Scam People Online*. It still hasn't arrived.

My friend claimed that he accidentally glued himself to his autobiography, but I don't believe him. However, that's his story and he's sticking to it.

Someone stole my thesaurus. I just can't put into words how angry I am.

***

CHILDREN

When I was a kid we had a quicksand box. I was an only child … eventually. – Steven Wright

Children certainly brighten up a home – they never turn the lights off.

I spent a lot of time, money and effort childproofing my house. But the kids still get in.

My wife is so negative. I remembered the car seat, the stroller *and* the nappy bag. Yet all she can talk about is how I forgot the baby.

Be nice to your children. They'll choose your care home.

Before having a child, the most important thing to ask yourself is: "Am I ready to watch the same cartoon on repeat for the next four years?"

I saw a sign that said "Watch for Children." I thought: "That sounds like a fair trade."

I tried to explain to my three-year-old grandson that it's perfectly normal to poop in your pants, but he still makes fun of me.

Having one child makes you a parent; having two makes you a referee.

If I was a wrestler with triplets I'd name them Niagara, Victoria and The Hunt for Red October, otherwise known as two falls and a sub mission.

A child's greatest period of growth is in the month after you've purchased new school clothes.

What's the one thing that children wear out faster than shoes? – Their parents.

I've got two wonderful children – and two out of five isn't bad.

How do you stop your children being spoiled? – Keep them in the fridge.

I like having conversations with kids. Adults never ask me what my third favourite reptile is.

Two children were deciding what game to play. "Let's play doctor," said one. "Good idea," said the other. "You operate and I'll sue."

My kids are very optimistic. Every glass they leave around the house is at least half full.

I have two boys, five and six. We're no good at naming things in our house. – Ed Byrne

***

CRIME

A man just assaulted me with milk, cream and butter. How dairy!

The police arrested two kids yesterday. One was drinking battery acid, the other was eating fireworks. They charged one and let the other off. – Tommy Cooper

The world champion tongue twister was arrested last week and given a really tough sentence.

A short fortune teller escaped from prison. Yes, a small medium is at large.

Airport police say that the number of people smuggling helium balloons in their luggage is under control. Nevertheless, cases continue to rise.

If you see a crime at an Apple store, does it make you an iWitness?

Two burglars stole a calendar. They each got six months.

I'd like to say to the man wearing camouflage gear and using crutches who stole my wallet at the weekend: "You can hide, but you can't run." – Milton Jones

A madman is on the loose after attacking six people with a knitting needle. The police think he may be following some kind of pattern.

While making their getaway, a gang of bank robbers crashed their car into a cement mixer. Police are looking for four hardened criminals.

A thief has been going around town stealing the wheels off police cars. Officers are working tirelessly to catch him.

Did you hear about the two peanuts walking in a rough neighbourhood? – One was a salted.

Crime in multi-storey car parks is wrong on so many different levels. – Tim Vine

***

DATING

I get very nervous on a first date, which is surprising as they are the only kind I have.

I usually meet my girlfriend at 12:59 because I like that one-to-one time. – Tom Ward

I asked my date to meet me at the gym, but she didn't show up. That's when I knew we weren't going to work out.

In college, I lived on a houseboat and started seeing the girl next door. Eventually we drifted apart.

Going to a bar on a singles night is like pushing your tray along in a cafeteria. Nothing looks good, but you know you have to pick something by the time you reach the cashier.

Speed dating is great because it would normally take months to have my hopes raised, then dashed, so many times.

Online dating helps me meet and break up with someone without having to leave the house.

I look great in my online dating profile pictures because they were taken when I didn't need online dating to meet people.

I avoid online dating sites because they match you up with people who share your interests. I don't want to go out with a weirdo.

I'm never using online dating again. The last guy said he lived in a gated community. It turned out to be prison.

I'll never join an online dating service because I prefer to meet someone the good, old-fashioned way ... through alcohol and poor judgement.

Recipes are like online dating websites. They never end up looking like the picture.

Afraid of not getting what you ordered with online shopping? – Wait until you try online dating.

***

DEATH

Will glass coffins prove to be a success? – Remains to be seen.

It's not the fall that kills you. It's the sudden stop at the end.

My dad died because he couldn't remember his blood type. As he was dying, he kept insisting we must "be positive", but it's tough now that he's not around.

The easiest job in the world has to be coroner. What's the worst thing that could happen? If everything goes wrong, maybe you'd get a pulse. – Dennis Miller

Police discovered the local ice cream man dead in his van and covered in raspberry sauce, nuts and hundreds and thousands. They think he topped himself.

I hope that when I inevitably choke to death on gummy bears, people will just say I was killed by bears and leave it at that.

I hate funerals. I'm not a mourning person.

How many men do you need for a Mafia funeral? – Just one, to slam the car boot shut.

The inventor of the throat lozenge died last month. There was no coffin at his funeral.

Old people at weddings always poke me and say, "You're next!" So I started doing the same thing to them at funerals.

My grandfather died of asbestosis. It took three months to cremate him.

Do I want to be buried or cremated? Oh, I don't know. Surprise me.

What do you call a dead magician? – An abracadaver.

Another World's Oldest Man has died. This is beginning to look suspicious.

Police have confirmed that the man who tragically fell from the roof of a fifteen-storey nightclub was not a bouncer.

The man who invented Velcro has died. RIP.

***

DEFINITIONS

A diplomat is someone who can tell you to go to hell in such a way that you look forward to the trip.

Hospitality: making your guests feel like they're at home, even if you wish they were.

When I was young, I asked my mother what a couple was. She said: "Two or three." And she wonders why her marriage didn't last!

Marriage is the triumph of imagination over intelligence. A second marriage is the triumph of hope over experience.

A husband is an attachment you screw on the bed to get the shelves put up.

Thanks so much for explaining the word "many" to me. It means a lot.

Laughing stock: cattle with a sense of humour.

A hangover is the wrath of grapes.

What is a Freudian slip? – When you say one thing, but mean your mother.

Depression is merely anger without enthusiasm.

Happiness: an agreeable sensation arising from contemplating the misery of another. – Ambrose Bierce

Impotence is nature's way of saying "no hard feelings".

What's the definition of an optimist? – A college student who opens his wallet and expects to find money.

So what if I don't know what Armageddon means? It's not the end of the world.

***

EDUCATION

On my first day at school my parents dropped me off at the wrong nursery. There I was … surrounded by shrubs and flowers.

When I went to school, sex education was mainly muttered warnings about the janitor. – Frankie Boyle

I received a call from the school telling me my son is constantly lying. I said: "Tell him he's a good liar. I don't have a son."

Teacher: "Johnny, you know you can't sleep in my class."
Pupil: "I know, Miss. But maybe if you were a little quieter I could."

Teacher: "Did your father help you with your homework last night?"
Pupil: "No, Miss. He did all of it."

Teacher: "I hope I didn't see you looking at Jimmy's test paper."
Pupil: "I hope you didn't see me, too."

Teacher: "For the last six months you've brought me a bag of raisins every week. Why have you stopped?"
Pupil: "My rabbit's dead, Miss."

Teacher: "I told you to stand at the end of the line."
Pupil: "I tried, but somebody was already there."

My teacher told me I'd never amount to anything because I procrastinate too much. I told her: "Just you wait."

If I got 50 pence for every maths exam I failed, I'd now have £4.30.

A student who changes the course of history is probably taking an exam.

My school was so posh that gym was called james.

Why did the teacher marry the janitor? – Because he swept her off her feet.

What did the math teacher do about his constipation problem? – He worked it out with a pencil.

I wanted to marry my English teacher when she got out of jail, but apparently you can't end a sentence with a proposition.

Why did the student eat his homework? – Because the teacher said it was a piece of cake.

I always say that boarding schools are run by therapists to turn out future clients. – Sandi Toksvig

How can you tell if you've been in college too long? – Your parents are running out of money.

In college, I was so broke I couldn't pay the electricity bill. Those were the darkest days of my life.

My college roommate was obsessed with trying to discover the largest known prime number. I wonder what he's up to now.

College is the opposite of kidnapping. They demand £100,000 from you or they'll send your kid back.

A graduation ceremony is an event where the speaker tells thousands of students dressed in identical caps and gowns that individuality is the key to success.

***

FAMILIES

Why are families like a box of chocolates? – They're mostly sweet, with a few nuts.

What's the best way to get in touch with your long-lost relatives? – Win the lottery.

I'll never forget what my late uncle said to me. He said: "I'm sorry I'm late."

About a month before he died, my grandfather had his back covered in lard. After that he went downhill fast.

What's the difference between an outlaw and an in-law? – Outlaws are wanted.

Understandably, my parents won't say which of their six kids they love the most, but they have told me I finished just out of the top five.

I'm very proud of my gold pocket watch. My grandfather, on his deathbed, sold me this watch. – Woody Allen

The family that sticks together should bathe more often.

I didn't know my road worker dad was a thief, but when I got home all the signs were there.

My dad didn't like me much. He only took me fishing once. I remember swimming back to shore and thinking …

Last Father's Day, my 24-year-old son gave me something I had been wanting for years: the keys to my car.

The reason grandparents and grandchildren get along so well is because they share a common enemy.

My grandfather has the heart of a lion and a lifetime ban from London Zoo.

I'm sure wherever my father is, he's looking down on us. He's not dead, just very condescending. – Jack Whitehall

***

FASHION

If you want to forget all your troubles, buy a pair of tight shoes.

I'm not sure whether I lost my camouflage pants or whether they're just doing a really good job.

Wearing a turtleneck is like getting strangled by a really weak guy all day. – Mitch Hedberg

Did you hear about the man who bought a jacket from a charity shop? – The only thing wrong with it was that one sleeve was slightly longer than the other two.

My wife was trying on different outfits yesterday and asked me what would make her dress look sexier. I said: "Give it to your sister."

I didn't think orthopaedic shoes would help, but I stand corrected.

I went into a clothing store and the lady asked me what size I was. I said: "Actually … I'm not to scale." – Demetri Martin

Why are there more organisations against fur clothing than against leather clothing? – Because it's easier to harass rich women than bikers.

I thought it was the new detergent we were using that was shrinking all my clothes, but it turned out to be the pizza place across the street.

Wear short sleeves – support your right to bare arms.

I bought a pair of jeans marked "50 per cent off". There was only one leg.

What do you know instantly about a well-dressed man? – His partner is good at picking out clothes.

My girlfriend is always borrowing my T-shirts and sweaters. But if I take one of her dresses, suddenly "we need to talk".

What did the tie say to the hat? – "You go on ahead and I'll hang around."

I saw a pair of knickers today. On the front it said "I would do anything for love" and on the back it said "but I won't do that". – Sarah Millican

My partner dresses to kill. She cooks the same way.

What did the bra say to the sock? – "I'll cover these two. You go on foot."

***

FISH

Two fish are in a tank. One says: "How do you drive this thing?"

Give a man a fish and you will feed him for a day. Teach a man to fish and he will spend a fortune on gear he will only use once a year.

I used to have a goldfish that could breakdance on the carpet … but only for about 10 seconds.

After a great birthday fishing and drinking with my friends, I came home to a very angry wife. Apparently, "Why don't you tie me to the bed and do whatever you want" had some caveats.

What did the fish say when he swam into the wall? – "Dam!"

What do you call a fish with no eyes? – A fsh.

Why did the fish get bad grades? – Because it was below C level.

What is the best way to communicate with a fish? – Drop it a line.

I went to see a play about fly fishing. The cast was excellent.

By way of experiment, a fisherman friend of mine used liquorice as bait. He caught all sorts.

***

FOOD AND DRINK

They demolished the local Domino's Pizza yesterday, and all the other shops in the street fell down.

I am not a vegetarian because I love animals. I am a vegetarian because I hate plants.

A lot of people cry when they cut onions. The trick is not to form an emotional bond.

My friends tell me that cooking is easy, but it's not easier than not cooking.

I read recipes the same way I read science fiction. I get to the end and I think: "Well, that's not going to happen."

I just had lunch at an excellent Christian restaurant called The Lord Giveth. They also do takeaways. – Tim Vine

I nearly dropped a plate of alphabetti spaghetti. That could have spelled disaster.

The best way to serve cabbage is to someone else.

Have you ever got halfway through eating a horse and thought: "I'm not as hungry as I thought I was"?

Why do the French eat snails? – They don't like fast food.

When two vegans get in an argument, is it still called a beef?

Did you hear about the haunted health food store? – Everything is super-natural.

I don't know why everyone keeps complaining about genetically modified food. I had a lovely leg of salmon the other day.

I used to eat a lot of natural foods until I learned that most people die of natural causes. – Jo Brand

Most children eat broccoli so that they'll grow up big and strong enough to be able to refuse it.

I was eating outside at a restaurant when it started raining. It took me an hour and a half to finish my soup.

How does Good King Wenceslas like his pizzas? – Deep pan, crisp and even.

Have you heard about the new restaurant called Karma? There are no main courses on the menu – just desserts.

I asked the waiter how they prepare their chickens. He said: "We just tell them straight that they're going to die."

My friend and I walked into a restaurant and the guy at the desk said: "Do you have reservations?" I said: "Yes, I expect the meat will be chewy and the vegetables overcooked."

"Waiter! What's this fly doing in my soup?"
"Looks like the backstroke, sir."

"Waiter! Why is your thumb on my steak?"
"I don't want it to fall on the floor again."

"Waiter! This coffee tastes like mud!"
"Yes, sir. It's fresh ground."

"Waiter! Coffee without cream, please."
"Sorry, sir, we're out of cream. Would you like it without milk?"

***

GIFTS

I bought my friend an elephant for his room. He said: "Thanks." I said: "Don't mention it."

I asked my wife what she wanted for her birthday. She said: "Nothing would make me happier than a diamond necklace." So I bought her nothing.

I love Christmas. I receive a lot of wonderful presents I can't wait to exchange. – Henny Youngman

I bought my wife a fridge for Christmas. I can't wait to see her face light up when she opens it.

Can you remember that awkward moment when you were about five years old and realised that Santa Claus was using the same wrapping paper as your parents?

How did Darth Vader know what Luke Skywalker was getting for Christmas? – He felt his presents.

Where is the best place to hide presents? – In the mouth of a gift horse.

I just received a letter informing me that my friend bequeathed me a very expensive antique watch. I really hope it's not a wind-up.

I went shopping the other day for a Christmas present and bought a barge pole. Thought I'd push the boat out.

There's nothing like the joy on a child's face at Christmas when he first sees the PlayStation box containing the socks I got him.

A friend bought a new wig before going on vacation. So I got him a comb as a parting gift.

I was given a new pair of gloves for my birthday, but they're both lefts, which, on the one hand is great, but on the other it's just not right.

I remember my aunt buying me a walkie-talkie for my sixth birthday. She said if I was good, she'd give me the other one for my seventh birthday.

My wife wasn't happy with the birthday present I bought her. She wanted something with diamonds; I got her a deck of cards.

***

HEALTH

I've just burned 2,000 calories. That's the last time I leave brownies in the oven while I nap.

I said to the gym instructor: "Can you teach me to do the splits?" He said: "How flexible are you?" I said: "I can't make Tuesdays." – Tommy Cooper

I have a friend who is addicted to brake fluid. He says he can stop any time.

I used to be addicted to soap, but I'm clean now.

I used to be addicted to the Hokey Cokey, but then I turned myself around.

It's easy to become addicted to helter-skelters. It's a downward spiral.

When I was a boy I had a disease that required me to eat dirt three times a day in order to survive. It's a good thing my older brother told me about it.

I entered what I ate today into my new health and fitness app. It just sent an ambulance to my house.

It's a scientific fact that birthdays are good for your health. The more of them you have, the longer you live.

My doctor told me that jogging could add years to my life. He was right – I feel 10 years older already.

I used to get heartburn when I ate birthday cake until a doctor advised me to take the candles off first.

Always make a point of befriending a recovering alcoholic. That way you'll never be short of a ride home.

The problem isn't that obesity runs in my family, it's that no one runs in my family.

My doctor told me I needed to break a sweat once a day, so I told him I'd start lying to my wife.

What does the Dentist of the Year receive? – A little plaque.

Why did the Buddhist monk refuse all the drugs he was offered at the dentist? – He wanted to transcend dental medication.

Why should you never heed the advice of dermatologists? – They make rash decisions.

Dad always said that laughter is the best medicine, which is probably why several of us died from tuberculosis.

I had a neck brace fitted a couple of years ago and I haven't looked back since.

My friend woke up this morning, spluttering and coughing. I think he may have pneumovasilibronchilichronotussidyspnoeichitis, but it's hard to say.

My doctor said that to improve my health I needed a new hobby that would get me outdoors more. So I took up smoking.

I went to my doctor and asked for something for persistent wind. He gave me a kite. – Les Dawson

I asked my doctor if he could give me something for my liver. He gave me half a pound of onions.

The worst time to have a heart attack is during a game of charades.

Who's the coolest person in a hospital? – The ultra sound guy.

And who stands in for him when he's on leave? – The hip replacement guy.

I just found out I'm colour blind. The diagnosis came completely out of the purple.

Who do you call when you need a doctor urgently? – The local golf club.

Why did the old lady slap the doctor around the face? – He told her she had acute angina.

As I left my car in the hospital car park, an attendant came over and said: "This is for badge holders only." I said: "But I've got a bad shoulder … "

I told my doctor that I'd broken my arm in two places. He told me to stop going to those places.

If four out of five people suffer from diarrhoea, does that mean there's one person who enjoys it?

There's a new Covid variant that makes you sweat peanut butter. It's okay, health officials are confident they can contain the spread.

There's a room at our local hospital where people sit around earnestly reading Scottish poetry. It's the Serious Burns Unit.

I went to see the doctor about my short-term memory problems. The first thing he did was make me pay in advance.

A doctor tells a woman she can no longer touch anything alcoholic. So she gets a divorce.

Doctor: "Your body has run out of magnesium."
Patient: "0Mg!"

Patient: "Doctor, my hair keeps falling out. Do you have anything to keep it in?"
Doctor: "How about a cardboard box?"

Patient: "I don't know what's wrong with me, doctor. I keep thinking I'm a pair of curtains."
Doctor: "Pull yourself together."

Patient: "Doctor, I can't stop stealing things."
Doctor: "Take these pills for a week and if they don't work, I'll have a flat-screen TV."

Receptionist: "Doctor, there's a man on the phone who says he's invisible."
Doctor: "Tell him I can't see him right now."

Nurse: "How is the little girl who swallowed the 50-pound note?"
Doctor: "No change yet."

Doctor to patient: "I have some good news and some bad news. But don't worry, I'll give the good news to your widow."

***

HISTORY

Who designed King Arthur's Round Table? – Sir Cumference.

Have you heard about the daredevil knight at Camelot? – Medieval Knievel.

Why did the knight run around shouting for a can opener? – He had a bee in his suit of armour.

What did Richard III say when a planning proposal was submitted for building a parking lot? – "Over my dead body!"

Why did Henry VIII have so many wives? – He liked to chop and change.

Where did Napoleon Bonaparte keep his armies? – Up his sleevies.

If Thomas Edison were alive today, what would he be most famous for? – Being 176 years old.

***

HOBBIES

I spent the last three days alone trying to learn escapology. I need to get out more.

God made rainy days so that gardeners could get the housework done.

I used to be afraid of gardening, but then I thought I'd grow a pear.

How do gardeners learn their craft? – By trowel and error.

As I suspected, someone has been adding soil to my garden. The plot thickens.

What's the difference between annual plants and perennials? – Annuals die every year and perennials die as soon as you get them home.

A friend of mine has a vegetable patch. It stops his cravings for carrots.

Don't tell secrets in the garden. The potatoes have eyes, the corn has ears and the beanstalk.

I saw Michael J. Fox in a gardening centre the other day. He had his back to the fuchsia.

If, instead of talking to your plants, you yelled at them, would they still grow, but be troubled and insecure?

My fake plants died because I forgot to pretend to water them.

What's red and smells like blue paint? – Red paint.

What did Tina Turner use to paint her kitchen? – Second-hand emulsion.

I was playing Bonopoly earlier. It's like Monopoly, but where the streets have no name.

It's hard to tell if people are interested in joining my Sarcastic Club or not. – Milton Jones

I was wondering why the Frisbee kept getting bigger and bigger, but then it hit me.

I'm going to combine my hobbies of taxidermy and bomb-making ... and make you an otter you can't defuse.

***

HOME

You know you live in a rough area when you buy an advent calendar and half of the windows are boarded up.

You know you're working class when your TV is bigger than your bookcase. – Rob Beckett

My aunt was so house-proud she used to put a sheet of newspaper under the cuckoo clock.

What's the best thing about living in Switzerland? – I don't know, but the flag is a big plus.

When I was a kid my parents moved house a lot, but I always found them.

How much does a new roof cost? – Nothing. It's on the house.

I gave an odd-job man a list of 10 things to do around the house, but he only did numbers one, three, five, seven and nine.

I read somewhere that 26 is too old to still live at home with your parents. It was on a note, in my room.

It's a five-minute walk from my house to the pub, but a 35-minute walk from the pub to my house. The difference is staggering.

I installed a skylight in my apartment. The people who live above me are furious.

The walls in our apartment are so thin, when I peel onions the neighbours cry.

I hate housework. You make the beds, you do the dishes – and six months later you have to start all over again. – Joan Rivers

My housekeeping style is best described as: "There appears to have been a struggle."

I had to ask my housemate Calvin to leave because he kept breaking the washing machine. Washing machines live longer with Cal gone.

***

INTELLIGENCE

My poor knowledge of Greek mythology has always been my Achilles' elbow.

I struggle with Roman numerals until I get to 159, then it just CLIX.

Intelligence is like underwear. It's important that you have it, but not necessary that you show it off.

Artificial intelligence is no match for natural stupidity.

A penny for some people's thoughts is still a fair price.

I used to think that the brain was the most wonderful organ in my body. Then I realised who was telling me this. – Emo Philips

Maybe if we start telling people their brain is an app, they'll want to use it.

Support bacteria – they're the only culture some people have.

Some come to the fountain of knowledge to drink; others prefer just to gargle.

What is the difference between intelligence and stupidity? – Intelligence has limits.

My work colleagues call me "The Computer". It has nothing to do with my intelligence – I just go to sleep if left unattended for 15 minutes.

Intelligence is the first thing I look for in a woman because if she doesn't have that, I may just have a chance.

As a scarecrow, people say I'm outstanding in my field. But hay, it's in my jeans.

***

INTERNET

When Dracula shops online, he keeps clicking on the button that says "Your account".

It's not always easy shopping on eBay. I searched for cigarette lighters and got over 10,000 matches.

I found a specialist site for toasters, but I had to give up after a while. There were too many pop-ups.

Before you marry a person, you should first make them use a computer with slow internet service to see who they really are. – Will Ferrell

In future I'm dating girls on Amazon, because they'll be sure to recommend other girls I might like.

I needed a password eight characters long. So I picked Snow White and the Seven Dwarfs.

I changed my password to "incorrect". So whenever I forget what it is, the computer will say, "Your password is incorrect."

Google is like my partner. It starts suggesting things before I can even finish my sentence.

Conjunctivitis.org: that's a site for sore eyes.

Did you hear about the guy who bought a rug on eBay that was advertised as being "in mint condition"? When it arrived, there was a big hole in the middle.

What goes "choo choo choo" while online? – Thomas the search engine.

What is Forrest Gump's internet password? – 1forrest1

The local tennis club's website is down. I think they are having problems with their server.

I love watching videos of running water on the internet. In fact, I'm watching a live stream right now.

I ordered a load of bubble wrap off eBay today – just to see what it gets delivered in. – Steven Wright

I asked my dad what his generation did to relieve boredom before the internet existed. Neither he nor any of my 19 siblings had an answer.

My wife is leaving me because I believe everything I read on the internet. I'm not worried because apparently there are plenty of sexy Russian girls living in my area.

Early to bed and early to rise is proof that you have lost your internet connection.

I bought a self-help DVD online. It was called *How to Handle Disappointment*. When I opened the box, it was empty.

They call it "surfing" the net. It's not surfing; it's typing in your bedroom. – Jack Dee

My internet password has been hacked. That's the third time I've had to rename the cat.

***

INVENTIONS

My grandfather invented the cold air balloon. It never really took off. – Milton Jones

The person who invented knock-knock jokes should get a no bell prize.

Why was the shovel regarded as one of the most notable inventions? – Because it was ground breaking.

What was more important than the invention of the first telephone? – The second telephone.

Which historical invention was the most revolutionary? – The wheel.

Before the invention of crowbars, crows had to drink at home.

If God had meant us to walk around naked, he would never have invented the wicker chair. – Erma Bombeck

***

LAWYERS

Talk is cheap – until you hire a lawyer.

Why did God make snakes just before lawyers? – To practise.

What do you call a lawyer with an IQ of 45? – Your Honour.

What do you call a lawyer gone bad? – Senator.

What's the difference between a lawyer and a pit bull? – Jewellery.

What is the difference between a lawyer and God? – God doesn't think he's a lawyer.

What's the difference between a good lawyer and a bad lawyer? – A bad lawyer can let a case drag on for several years. A good lawyer can make it last even longer.

What's the difference between a good lawyer and a great lawyer? – A good lawyer knows the law, a great lawyer knows the judge.

When lawyers die, why are they buried 500 feet underground? – Because deep down, they're really nice people.

What's the difference between a lawyer and a vampire? – A vampire only sucks blood at night.

What do you call a smiling, sober, courteous person at a Bar Association convention? – The caterer.

Why is it so common for lawyers to be lost in thought? – Unfamiliar territory.

Copper wire was invented by two lawyers fighting over a penny.

Why won't sharks attack lawyers? – Professional courtesy.

What are 15 skydiving lawyers called? – Skeet.

Did you hear about the new microwave lawyer? – You spend eight minutes in his office and get billed as if you'd been there eight hours.

The trouble with the legal profession is that 98 per cent of its members give the rest a bad name.

Why is it unethical for lawyers to sleep with their clients? – To stop the client being billed twice for the same service.

I broke a mirror the other day – that's seven years bad luck. My lawyer thinks he can get me five.

Arriving at the scene of a car crash, a paramedic asked the driver: "Are you badly hurt?"
"I don't know," said the driver. "I haven't spoken to my lawyer yet."

***

LIGHT BULB JOKES

How many lawyers does it take to change a light bulb? – None. They'd rather keep their clients in the dark.

How many psychiatrists does it take to change a light bulb? – Only one, but the bulb really has to want to change.

How many actors does it take to change a light bulb? – Only one. They don't like to share the spotlight.

How many mystery writers does it take to change a light bulb? – Two. One to screw it almost all the way in and then one to give it a surprising twist at the end.

How many airline pilots does it take to change a light bulb? – One. He just holds it while the world revolves around him.

How many police officers does it take to change a light bulb? – None, because it will turn itself in.

How many economists does it take to change a light bulb? – None. If the light bulb needed changing, the market would already have done it.

How many computer programmers does it take to change a light bulb? – None. It's a hardware problem.

How many folk musicians does it take to change a light bulb? – Five. One to change the bulb and four to complain about going electric.

How many jazz musicians does it take to change a light bulb? – A-one, a-two, a-one-two-three-four.

How many performance artists does it take to change a light bulb? – No one knows because no one stays until the end.

***

MEN

What do anniversaries and toilets have in common? – Men keep missing them.

Men have two emotions: hungry and horny. If you see him without an erection, make him a sandwich.

Behind every angry woman is a man who has absolutely no idea what he did wrong.

Few women admit their age; few men act it.

Why are men like placemats? – Because they only appear when there's food on the table.

Why are men like mascara? – Because they run at the first sign of emotion.

Why are men like lava lamps? – Because they're fun to look at, but they're not very bright.

Men do cry, but only when assembling furniture. – Rita Rudner

How do men exercise on the beach? – By sucking in their stomachs every time they see a bikini.

A retired husband is often a wife's full-time job.

For a man, what is the downside of a threesome? – He'll probably disappoint two women instead of one.

How does a man show that he's planning for the future? – He buys two cases of beer instead of one.

What's a man's idea of a seven-course meal? – A hot dog and a six-pack.

When is the only time a man thinks about a candlelit dinner? – When there's been a power cut.

Why do men whistle while they're sitting on the toilet? – It helps them to remember which end they need to wipe.

How do men sort their laundry? – Filthy and Filthy but Wearable.

Women sometimes make fools of men, but most guys are the do-it-yourself type.

There are only two four-letter words that are offensive to men: "don't" and "stop", unless they are used together.

Why do men like smart women? – Opposites attract.

What makes men chase women they have no intention of marrying? – The same urge that makes dogs chase cars they have no intention of driving.

What's a man's idea of foreplay? – Half an hour of begging.

What do you call a man who's just had sex? – Anything you like; he's asleep.

I don't hate men. I think men are absolutely fantastic … as a concept. – Jo Brand

What's the difference between a g-spot and a golf ball? – Men will spend 20 minutes looking for a golf ball.

Moses was leading his people through the desert for 40 years. It seems even in Biblical times, men refused to ask for directions.

What should you give a man who has everything? – A woman to show him how to work it.

Why do men prefer electric lawnmowers? – So they can find their way back to the house.

Behind every great man is a woman rolling her eyes.

***

MIDDLE AGE

Middle age is when you're faced with two temptations and you choose the one that will get you home by nine o'clock.

Middle age is when you start turning out the lights for economic rather than romantic reasons.

Middle age is when broadness of the mind and narrowness of the waist change places.

Middle age is when work is a lot less fun and fun is a lot more work.

What's the difference between a clown and a man having a mid-life crisis? – The clown *knows* he's wearing ridiculous clothes.

My mother used to say: "40 is the new 30." Lovely woman … banned from driving.

***

MILITARY

How can you tell if someone was in the military? – Give them five minutes and they'll tell you themselves.

How do different military branches use stars? – The army sleeps under the stars. The navy navigates by the stars. The air force chooses hotels by the stars.

The man who survived both mustard gas and pepper spray is now a seasoned veteran.

What do you get if you drop a piano on a military base? – A flat major.

Did you hear about the accident on base? – A tank ran over a box of popcorn and squashed four kernels.

Did you hear about the karate master who joined the military? – He saluted and nearly chopped off his own head.

Why are soldiers always tired on 1 April? – Because they just had a 31-day March.

You can now be fined £700 for calling an officer an idiot. Fifty pounds for calling them an idiot and £650 for disclosing classified information.

How do you know when your date with a fighter pilot is nearly over? – He says: "Enough about me. Want to hear about my plane?"

In the navy, how do you separate the men from the boys? – With a crowbar.

Why couldn't the sailors play cards? – The captain was sitting on the deck.

A guy in our unit could balance a ball on the end of his nose. I said: "Let me guess: you were in the Seals?"

What do you call a Marine with an IQ of 160? – A platoon.

Why did God give the Marine one more brain cell than the horse? – So he wouldn't poop along the parade route.

Can someone please tell me what the lowest rank in the army is? Every time I ask someone, they say it's private.

***

MONEY

Always borrow money from a pessimist. He won't expect it back.

I decided to sell my Hoover because all it was doing was gathering dust. – Tim Vine

A man knocked on my door today and asked for a small donation towards the local swimming pool. I gave him a glass of water.

I won three million dollars on the lottery this weekend, so I decided to give a quarter to charity. Now I have $2,999,999.75.

I asked the bank teller to check my balance. So she pushed me over.

Living on Earth is expensive, but it does include a free trip around the sun.

I saw a homeless guy on the street with a sign that said "One day this could be you". So I put my money back in my pocket, just in case he's right.

I used to live hand to mouth. Do you know what changed my life? Cutlery. – Tim Vine

The business plan for my new shadow puppet theatre says we'll make a fortune, but those are just projected figures.

Money isn't everything, but it certainly keeps you in touch with your children.

Money can't buy you true love. It does, however, put you in a good bargaining position.

Money can't buy you friends, but you do get a better class of enemy. – Spike Milligan

Being poor has its advantages. For example, your keys are never in your other trousers.

Why did God create stock market analysts? – To make weather forecasters look good.

Swimming with sharks cost me an arm and a leg.

With great power comes a great electricity bill.

Recently I spent £750 to hire a limousine and then realised that's just for the car, not the driver. Hard to believe I've spent all that money, but have nothing to chauffeur it.

***

MUSIC

At any given moment the urge to sing "The Lion Sleeps Tonight" is just a whim away, a whim away, a whim away.

I told my friend I like Beyoncé. "Whatever floats your boat," she said. I said: "No, that's buoyancy."

My friend got me a ruler from Smiths. Heaven knows I'm measurable now.

I went to see The Clash, but there was another band on at the same time.

The Jam and Cream were both going to reform to play a series of gigs in Devon and Cornwall, but they couldn't agree who should go on first.

With the rise of self-driving vehicles, it is surely just a matter of time before we get a country song where a guy's truck leaves him too.

A friend of mine is a musician. He used to be in a band called The Hinges. They were quite big. They supported The Doors.

Some other friends of mine were in a band called The Prevention. They were better than The Cure.

I went to see Placebo once. I actually thought they were The Cure.

Did you hear about the orchestra that was hit by lightning? – Only the conductor died.

What's the difference between a drummer and a pigeon? – A pigeon can still make a deposit on a Mercedes.

What do you call someone who hangs around with musicians? – A drummer.

How can you tell if a singer's at your door? – They can't find the key and don't know when to come in.

How do you get a musician off your porch? – Pay for the pizza.

What's an accordion good for? – Learning how to fold maps.

What do a cello and a lawsuit have in common? – Everyone is relieved when the case is closed.

What's the difference between a cello and an onion? – No one cries when you chop up a cello.

The worst thing I ever bought for my car was a Bonnie Tyler sat nav. It keeps telling me to turn around, and every now and then it falls apart.

My definition of an intellectual is someone who can listen to the *William Tell* Overture without thinking of *The Lone Ranger*. – Billy Connolly

I once stayed in a haunted house that kept playing old disco classics. At first I was afraid, I was petrified.

I used to think Elton John's favourite salad vegetable was lettuce. Then I remembered that he's more of a rocket man.

How do you turn a duck into a soul singer? – Put it in a microwave until its Bill Withers.

How do you annoy Lady Gaga? – Poker face.

Why did Bono fall off the stage? – He was too close to The Edge.

How do you make a bandstand? – Take away their chairs.

How does Bob Marley like his donuts? – Wi' jammin'.

Two wind turbines in a field were discussing their favourite type of music. Both were huge metal fans.

I fainted in the curry house when I heard that R.E.M. had split up. That's me in the korma.

Two of the Beach Boys walk into a bar. "Round?" "Round." "Get a round?" "I'll get a round."

How do you work out how heavy a red hot chili pepper is? – Give it a weigh, give it a weigh, give it a weigh now.

What concert costs just 45 cents? – 50 Cent featuring Nickelback.

I phoned up to book tickets for an Elvis tribute act. The automated voice told me to press one for the money, two for the show …

***

MYSTERIES

How is it that one careless match can start a forest fire, but it takes a whole box to start a campfire?

If you're not supposed to eat at night, why is there a light in the refrigerator?

If money doesn't grow on trees, how come banks have branches?

Why is the time of day with the slowest traffic called rush hour?

How do you know when you've run out of invisible ink?

Why doesn't super glue stick to the inside of the tube?

If nothing sticks to Teflon, how does Teflon stick to the pan?

If one synchronised swimmer drowns, do the rest have to drown too?

If swimming is so good for your figure, how come whales are fat?

If practice makes perfect and nobody's perfect, then why practise?

Why is there only one Monopolies Commission?

Why do they never sell car boots at car boot sales?

Are people born with photographic memories or does it take time to develop?

Why isn't the word "phonetic" spelt the way it sounds?

If you don't pay your exorcist, do you get repossessed?

How does the guy who drives the snowplough get to work?

What should you do if you see an endangered animal eating an endangered plant?

Before they invented drawing boards, what did they go back to?

If a man overdoses on Viagra, how do they get the coffin lid shut?

What if there were no hypothetical questions?

How do "Do Not Walk on the Grass" signs get there?

Why does someone believe you when you say there are 400 billion stars, but check when you say the paint is wet?

Smoking will kill you. Bacon will kill you. And yet smoking bacon will cure it.

***

OLD AGE

What did the pirate say when he turned 80 years old? – "Aye, matey."

Old age is when you are cautioned to slow down by your doctor instead of the police.

Old age is when you stoop to pick something up and try to think of other things you can do while you're down there.

Old age is when it takes longer to rest than it did to get tired.

Old age is when "getting lucky" means finding your car in the parking lot.

I'm at an age when my back goes out more than I do. – Phyllis Diller

I'm at the age when I can't take anything with a pinch of salt.

You know you're old when people call at 9.30 p.m. and ask: "Did I wake you?"

When you get old, safe sex means not falling out of bed.

I'm at the age where I have to make a noise when I bend over. It's the law.

The older a man gets, the farther he had to walk to school as a boy.

My grandfather's 81, but he can still cut the mustard. He just needs help opening the jar.

Even at that age, my grandfather is a three-times-a-night man. He really shouldn't drink so much tea before going to bed.

My grandfather keeps a record of everything he eats. It's called a tie.

Nostalgia is heroin for old people. – Dara Ó Briain

I'm having a great day. Woke up this morning, got out of bed, went to the bathroom. In that order!

***

PARTIES

At every party there are two types of people: those who want to go home and those who don't. The trouble is they are usually married to each other.

Nothing embarrasses a psychic more than a surprise party.

I didn't want to go to the 1980s-music-themed party, but my friend was adamant.

A police officer accidentally arrested a judge who was dressed like a convict for a fancy dress party. He quickly learned never to book a judge by their cover.

Going to a party with your wife is like going fishing with a game warden.

I went to a postman's birthday party last week. We played "pass the 'sorry you weren't in' note".

I went to a seafood party last week, but ended up pulling a mussel.

I was about to go to a fancy dress party as a can of deodorant. My wife stopped me and said: "Are you Sure?"

I went to a Halloween party dressed as Dracula and ate all the food. I was Vampire the Buffet Slayer.

When I moved into my igloo, my friends threw me a house-warming party. Now I'm homeless.

After my son's football team won their league, the goalkeeper invited the two of us to a party at his house. It was the Father, the Son and the Goalie Host.

***

PERSONALITY

My three favourite things are eating my family and not using commas.

My friend is a procrastinator. He didn't get his birthmark until he was eight years old. – Steven Wright

I can totally keep secrets. It's the people I tell them to who can't.

A positive attitude may not solve all your problems. But it will annoy enough people to make it worth the effort.

I went to the annual meeting of the Society of Pessimists. It was very disappointing. The room was half-empty.

My therapist says I have a preoccupation with vengeance. We'll see about that. – Stewart Francis

I have an inferiority complex, but it's not a very good one.

What is it that even the most careful person overlooks? – Their nose.

Those are my principles. If you don't like them, I have others. – Groucho Marx

People say I've got no willpower, but I've quit smoking loads of times.

Some people think I have a split personality. To them I say: "No, he doesn't."

I'm the kind of guy who doesn't take orders from anyone, which is probably why I lost my job as a waiter.

Honesty may be the best policy, but it's important to remember that apparently, by elimination, dishonesty is the second-best policy. – George Carlin

My girlfriend and I often laugh about how competitive we are. But I laugh more.

***

POLICE

Why did the policeman stay in bed all day? – He was an undercover officer.

Thieves broke into a police station and stole all the toilets. The police say they have nothing to go on.

The police are saying I assaulted a guy with a sheet of sandpaper. All I did was rough him up a bit.

How many police officers does it take to break an egg? – None. "It fell down the stairs."

Do I lose when the police officer says "papers" and I say "scissors"?

I find it ironic that the colours red, white and blue stand for freedom until they are flashing behind you.

If the police arrest a mime artist, do they tell him he has the right to remain silent?

A large hole appeared in the road outside our local police station. The police say they are looking into it.

We live in a society where pizza gets to your house before the police.

This policeman came up to me with a pencil and a piece of very thin paper. He said: "I want you to trace someone for me." – Tim Vine

Someone stole four dogs from a dog walker yesterday. The police have no leads.

I got pulled over by the police last night. They asked me where I was between 7 and 11. I said I was in junior school.

Why do police officers get to protests early? – To beat the crowd.

A week after my wife went missing, the police told me I should expect the worst-case scenario. So I went back to the charity shop and retrieved all her old clothes.

***

POLITICS

What do you get when you ask a politician to tell "the truth, the whole truth and nothing but the truth"? – Three different answers.

How can you tell when politicians are lying? – Their lips are moving.

Why don't politicians like golf? – Because it's too much like their work; trapped in one bad lie after another.

Honesty in politics is much like oxygen. The higher up you go, the scarcer it becomes.

Definition of an honest politician: one who, once bought, will stay bought.

A statesman is any politician it's considered safe to name a school after. – Bill Vaughan

You can always count on politicians to do the right thing – after they've tried everything else.

Politicians are people who divide their time between running for office and running for cover.

Politicians and nappies have one thing in common. Both should be changed regularly, and for the same reason.

***

RELATIONSHIPS

Did you hear about the woman who decided to sleep on her husband's side of the bed for a change, because apparently from that side you don't hear the children wake up at night?

What's the difference between a new husband and a new dog? – After a year, the dog is still excited to see you.

My wife has kicked me out because of my bad Arnold Schwarzenegger impressions. But don't worry … I'll return.

My wife arrived home to find me dozing on the sofa next to a bench tool stand. She immediately accused me of sleeping with a Workmate.

I'm single by choice. Not my choice.

Despite the contradictory advice circulated in the late 1990s, if you wanna be my lover, please do not get with my friends.

Losing a husband can be hard. In my case, it was almost impossible.

Marriage is the only war where you sleep with the enemy.

My husband and I were inseparable. Sometimes it took four people to pull us apart.

My wife and I have been married 22 years – 46 with the windchill factor.

You may marry the man of your dreams, ladies, but 14 years later you're married to a couch that burps. – Roseanne Barr

If it weren't for marriage, men would go through life thinking they had no faults at all.

When a woman steals your husband, there is no better revenge than to let her keep him.

Do you know what the most important thing is in a relationship? Trust. Because if you don't trust your lover, how do you know he's not going to tell your partner?

My girlfriend said: "You act too much like a detective. I want to split up." "Good idea," I replied. "We can cover more ground that way."

Did you hear about the cannibal who dumped her boyfriend?

I just ended a long-term relationship today. I'm not too bothered. It wasn't mine.

What's a man's idea of honesty in a relationship? – Telling you his real name.

My wife keeps complaining I never listen to her … or something like that.

A husband is someone who, when he takes out the trash, gives the impression that he has just cleaned the whole house.

Not all men want a relationship just for sex. Some want their washing done too.

Marriage is like going to a restaurant. You order what you want, then when you see what the other person has, you wish you had ordered that.

Marriage is the process of finding out what kind of man your wife would have preferred.

When a man opens the door of his car for his wife, you can be sure of one thing: either the car is new or the wife is.

I once gave my husband the silent treatment for an entire week, at the end of which he declared: "Hey, we're getting along pretty great lately!" – Bonnie McFarlane

She wanted a puppy. But I didn't want a puppy. So we compromised and got a puppy.

Funny how they say, "We need to talk," when they really mean, "You need to listen."

A smart husband is one who thinks twice before saying nothing.

I haven't spoken to my wife for 18 months. I don't like to interrupt her.

When a man holds a woman's hand before marriage, it's love; after marriage, it's self-defence.

To some, marriage is just a word; to others, it's a sentence.

A happily married man is one who understands every word his wife didn't say.

When I'm not in a relationship I shave one leg so it feels like I'm sleeping with a woman.

I would never ever cheat in a relationship, because that would require two people to find me attractive.

I love being married. It's so great to find that one special person you want to annoy for the rest of your life. – Rita Rudner

My girlfriend and I just transitioned to a long-distance relationship. Or, as she likes to call it, a "restraining order".

My boyfriend said he was leaving me because he couldn't handle my OCD. I told him five times to close the door on his way out.

Every person in a long-term relationship should forget their mistakes. There's no point in two people remembering the same thing.

A good wife is one who always forgives her husband when she's wrong.

Relationships are a lot like algebra. Have you ever looked at your X and wondered Y?

My wife is threatening to leave me because of my obsession with acting like a TV news anchor. More on this after the break.

***

RELIGION

How do you get holy water? – Boil the hell out of it.

What do you get when you mix holy water with laxatives? – A religious movement.

A true test of faith is when the collection plate comes around and you only have a £20 note.

As far as I'm concerned, the scariest thing to come out of the Muslim world is algebra. – Rob Delaney

Jesus walked into a hotel, handed the receptionist a box of nails and said: "Can you put me up for the night?"

There's a new gym in town catering solely for religious people. It's called Jehovah's Fitness.

Going to church does not make you a Christian any more than standing in a garage makes you a car.

Did you hear about the church janitor who was also the organist? – He had to watch his keys and pews.

I was christened by a vicar in a gorilla suit. It was a blessing in disguise.

What do you call a religious organisation that doesn't make any money? – Non-prophet.

Adam and Eve were the first ones to ignore the Apple terms and conditions.

How do we know Adam was a Baptist? – Only a Baptist could stand next to a naked woman and be tempted by a piece of fruit.

Why don't Baptists make love standing up? – Because it could lead to dancing.

Bishops tried to take a step forward by introducing female bishops. It failed. Everyone knows bishops can only move diagonally. – Jimmy Carr

Two priests decided to open a fish and chip shop. One was a fish friar, the other was a chip monk.

What do priests and Christmas trees have in common? – The balls are just for decoration.

Why didn't Noah swat those two mosquitoes?

Nun: "There's a case of syphilis in the convent."
Mother Superior: "Good, I was getting tired of the Chardonnay."

And the Lord said unto John: "Come forth and receive eternal life." But John came fifth and won a toaster.

***

SCIENCE

The adjective for metal is metallic, but not so for iron, which is ironic.

Photons have mass? I didn't even know they were Catholic.

Scientists have recently found the gene for shyness. They would have found it earlier, but it was hiding behind two other genes.

Why are robots never afraid? – Because they have nerves of steel.

If you break the Law of Gravity, do you get a suspended sentence?

Why should you never trust atoms? – They make up everything.

Did you hear oxygen went on a date with potassium? It went OK.

What did one tectonic plate say when it bumped into another? – Sorry, my fault.

Did you hear about the microbiologist who put on weight? – He's now a biologist.

A nuclear physicist is someone who has many ions in the fire.

What is a quark? – The sound a posh duck makes.

***

SEX

I once had sex for an hour and five minutes. I'll always remember it because it was the night the clocks went forward.

Sometimes when I'm having sex, I'm already thinking about what I'm going to write in the thank-you letter. – Holly Walsh

The only time my ex didn't fake an orgasm was when the judge signed the divorce papers.

Why is sex like a game of bridge? – If you have a good hand, you don't need a partner.

My girlfriend asked me to name all the women I've slept with. I probably should have stopped when I got to her.

I asked my wife why she never blinked during foreplay. She said she didn't have time.

Foreplay is like beef burgers – three minutes on each side. – Victoria Wood

I bought some of those super-sensitive condoms. They're great. They hang around afterwards and murmur sweet nothings.

There's a new addition to the *Kama Sutra*. It's called the plumber position: you stay in all day and nobody comes.

The nurse at the sperm bank asked me if I'd like to masturbate in the cup. I said: "Well, I'm pretty good, but I don't think I'm ready to compete just yet."

Last night our sex was so good that even the neighbours had a cigarette.

All my mother told me about sex was that the man goes on top and the woman on the bottom. For three years my husband and I slept in bunk beds. – Joan Rivers

I think my girlfriend must have had 61 boyfriends before me because she calls me her 60-second lover.

I organised a threesome for last night. There were a couple of no-shows, but I still had fun.

***

SHOPPING

When you've seen one shopping centre, you've seen a mall.

I went to the paper shop this morning, but it had blown away.

A bargain is something you don't need at a price you can't resist.

Ever since buying a digital camera, I can only think of it in positive terms. There are no negatives.

I walked up to the cheese counter … which interrupted him and so he had to start again.

I bought a new airplane last week. I was disappointed they wouldn't let me keep the hangar.

My wife is a compulsive shopper. She will buy anything marked down. Once she came home with an escalator. – Henny Youngman

My wife asked me to put ketchup on the shopping list I was making and now I can't read any of it.

Last week I bought a fridge magnet. They really work. So far I've got 11 fridges.

I ordered a chicken and an egg from Amazon. I'll let you know.

**

SLEEP

I'm really good at sleeping. I can do it with my eyes closed.

If you want your partner to pay undivided attention to every word you say, talk in your sleep.

Did you hear about the couple who bought a water bed? – They soon drifted apart.

How do you make a water bed more bouncy? – Use spring water.

My wife just found out I replaced our bed with a trampoline. She hit the roof!

I sleep better naked. I just wish the flight attendant had been more understanding.

Sometimes I wake up grumpy. Other times I let him sleep.

I was struggling to sleep at night, so I went to a therapist for advice. He said: "Sleep on the edge of the bed. You'll soon drop off."

I woke up this morning and forgot which side the sun rises from. Then it dawned on me.

Why do women rub their eyes when they get up in the morning? – Because they don't have balls to scratch.

I dreamed I wrote *The Hobbit* the other night. I think I was Tolkien in my sleep.

***

SOCIAL MEDIA

What's the opposite of social media? – Social life.

Instagram is just Twitter for people who go outside.

I used to like to think of something really stupid to say, but not actually say it. Then along came Twitter ...

Jesus is on Twitter, but he's only got 12 followers.

A Chinese social media platform has been accused of poisoning breath mints to achieve global domination. Commentators have called it the TikTok tic tac tactic.

Social media was down today, so I left my room and met my family. They seem pretty cool.

***

SPORTS

Golf is a game invented by God to punish people who retire early.

It takes a lot of balls to play golf the way I do.

I once played a course that was so tough, I lost two balls in the ball washer.

Golf scores are directly proportional to the number of witnesses.

The only reason I play golf is to annoy my wife. She thinks I'm having fun.

The position of your hands is very important when playing golf. I use mine to cover up my scorecard.

Golf is a test of your skill against your opponent's luck.

If your opponent has trouble remembering whether he shot a six or a seven, he probably shot an eight.

Why did the golfer wear two pairs of pants? – In case he got a hole in one.

The secret of good golf is to hit the ball hard, straight and not too often.

A "gimme" can best be defined as an agreement between two golfers, neither of whom can putt very well.

Golf balls are like eggs. They're white, they're sold by the dozen, and a week later you have to buy some more.

Practice tee: a place where golfers go to convert a nasty hook into a wicked slice.

The best wood in most golfers' bags is the pencil.

I set out to shoot my age, but I shot my weight instead.

The man who takes up golf to get his mind off work soon takes up work to get his mind off golf.

The reason the golf pro tells you to keep your head down is so you can't see him laughing. – Phyllis Diller

Playing golf the other day I broke 70. That's a lot of clubs.

An interesting thing about golf is that no matter how badly you play, it's always possible to get worse.

"I ran a half marathon" sounds so much better than "I quit halfway through a marathon".

They used to time me with a stopwatch. Now they use a calendar.

What's harder to catch the faster you run? – Your breath.

My Czech mate is surprisingly bad at chess.

I was playing chess with my friend and he said: "Let's make this interesting." So we stopped playing chess. – Matt Kirshen

I tried water polo, but my horse drowned.

I often get a 147 when I play snooker. It's the number of the bus that stops outside the hall.

I like telekinetic snooker, but you do have to be in the right frame of mind.

Why are there so many baseball autobiographies? – Because every pitcher tells a story.

What is the difference between New York Yankees fans and dentists? – One roots for the yanks, the other yanks for the roots.

A bad football team is like an old bra – no cups and little support.

After dating the team's goalie for a while, my sister decided he was definitely a keeper.

How did the football pitch end up as a triangle? – Somebody took a corner.

Why did the soccer coach flood the pitch? – He wanted to bring on a sub.

Why did women's football take so long to catch on? – Because it took ages to persuade 11 women to wear the same outfit in public.

Racecar backwards is still racecar. Racecar upside down is expensive.

I don't trust skiing as a sport. Its i's are too close together.

I received a useful pamphlet with my new skis. It tells you how to convert them into a pair of splints.

Why should you never marry a tennis player? – Because love means nothing to them.

The depressing thing about tennis is that no matter how good I get, I'll never be as good as a wall. They're so relentless. – Mitch Hedberg

Where is the first tennis match mentioned in the Bible? – When Joseph served in Pharaoh's court.

Why was Cinderella so bad at sports? – Because she had a pumpkin for a coach.

You don't need a parachute to go skydiving. You need a parachute to go skydiving *twice*.

***

TECHNOLOGY

Whoever said technology would replace all paper obviously hasn't tried wiping their butt with an iPad.

There are only two types of computer: the latest model and the obsolete.

A computer once beat me at chess, but it was no match for me at kickboxing. – Emo Philips

What's the difference between a car salesman and a computer salesman? – The car salesman *knows* he's lying.

A clean house is the sign of a broken computer.

Computers are like air conditioners. They stop working when you open Windows.

I wondered why music was coming from my computer printer. Apparently the paper was jamming.

I asked the IT guy: "How do you make a motherboard?" He said: "I tell her about my job."

What is a cursor? – Someone who is having problems with their computer.

Our work computers went down yesterday, so we had to do everything manually. It took me 15 minutes to shuffle the cards for solitaire.

Isn't it great to live in the 21st century, when deleting history has become more important than making it?

I bought a new shrub trimmer last week. It's cutting hedge technology.

Did you hear about the guy who put airbags on his first computer in case it crashed?

I'm moving with the times, embracing new technology. Instead of going into a room and forgetting what I was looking for, I now log onto Google and forget what I was searching for.

I used to work in restaurants before switching to a job in IT. The biggest difference is that the phrase "my server went down on me" is no longer a good thing.

People who use selfie sticks really need to have a good, long look at themselves.

I want to be something really scary for Halloween this year, so I'm dressing up as a phone battery at two per cent.

Anyone who thinks talk is cheap obviously didn't pay my daughter's last mobile phone bill.

Two mobile phones got married. The wedding was lousy, but the reception was amazing.

Why did Jack and Jill *really* go up the hill? – To get better wifi.

My grandfather said the younger generation rely too much on technology. So I called him a hypocrite and unplugged his life support.

I like an escalator because an escalator can never break. It can only become stairs. – Mitch Hedberg

What did the digital clock say to the grandfather clock? –
"Look, Grandpa, no hands!"

***

TEENAGERS

I'm not sure whether growing pains are something
teenagers have – or are.

What's the best way to keep a teenage boy out of hot
water? – Put some dishes in it.

A teenager is someone whose hang-ups don't include
clothes.

Adolescence is a time of rapid change. Between the ages
of 13 and 19, a parent can age as much as 20 years.

Teenagers are incredibly well-informed about any subject
they don't have to study.

There's nothing wrong with teenagers that reasoning
with them won't aggravate.

***

TEXTING

Arguing with autocorrect is the new yelling at the television.

Autocorrect has become my worst enema.

Thanks to autocorrect, one in five children will be getting a visit from Satan this Christmas.

You know you're texting too much when you're happy to stop at a red light.

I almost got into an accident with someone who was texting while driving. Luckily, I braked just in time or I would have spilled my beer.

I'm old enough to remember when emojis were called hieroglyphics.

The person who invented autocorrect passed away today. Restaurant in peace.

***

TRAVEL

My wife wanted to go on vacation, but I wanted a staycation. So we compromised and had an altercation.

I've just been on a once-in-a-lifetime holiday. I'll tell you what, never again. – Tim Vine

I went to the Isle of Dogs once. Apparently it's the Isle of Man's best friend.

I just told my suitcases we aren't going on holiday this year. Now I'm having to deal with emotional baggage.

My friend insisted that we go to Stockholm on holiday. I didn't want to go at first, but now I don't want to leave.

My wife and I can never agree on holidays. I want to go to exotic islands and stay in five-star hotels. She wants to come with me.

I bought my wife a world map and gave her a dart. I told her to throw it and wherever it lands, we will go on holiday. So this year we're spending two weeks behind the fridge.

My wife told me: "Sex is better on holiday." That wasn't a very nice postcard to receive. – Joe Bor

I checked into a hotel and asked for an early morning wake-up call. At 7am the receptionist rang and said: "What are you doing with your life?"

If you look like your passport photo, you're probably not well enough to travel.

Did you hear about the American tourist who was surprised they built Windsor Castle directly under the flight path to Heathrow?

I asked my North Korean friend how it was there. He said he couldn't complain.

Last week, I went on a trip to a postcard factory. It was okay, nothing to write home about.

A friend said: "You want to go to Brighton, it's good for rheumatism." So I did and I got it. – Tommy Cooper

I once stayed in a posh hotel with towels so thick I could barely shut my suitcase.

I went up to the airport information desk and asked: "How many airports are there in the world?"

I asked the flight attendant: "Does this type of plane crash often?" She said: "No, only once."

The purpose of the airplane propeller is to keep the pilot cool. If you don't believe me, stop the propeller and watch the pilot sweat.

Did you hear about the man who only rode the New York subway to have his clothes pressed?

I was out cycling and someone told me that one of my mud flaps had fallen off. I said I'd carry on rear guardless.

My grandfather was on a ship that sank on November 5. He let off all the flares, but the people on the other ships just went, "Ooooh! Aaaah!"

Think twice before boarding a cruise ship where the passengers are supplied with oars.

Can't help feeling my ostrich friend isn't making the most of our trip to the beach. – Milton Jones

Did you hear that the highways maintenance department is laying off hundreds of workers? Someone has invented a shovel that stands up by itself.

As one door closes, another one opens. That's the last time I buy a used car online.

My car broke down on the motorway and reduced me to tears. At least I had a hard shoulder to cry on.

Did you hear about the guy who had a personalised number plate BAA BAA? He had a black Jeep.

How did the driver get a puncture? – He didn't see the fork in the road.

I bought a Swiss car. It runs like clockwork, but I can't figure out how to get it out of neutral.

I bought a car from a little old lady who only drove it on Sundays … when she took it to demolition derbies.

Every time my car passes a scrapyard it gets homesick.

A careful driver is one who has just spotted a speed camera.

What's the most dangerous part of a car? – The nut behind the wheel.

I took my car for a service last week. It was a real struggle getting it into the church.

My husband had his driving test last week. He got eight out of ten. The other two guys jumped clear.

Apparently I snore so loudly it scares everyone in the car I'm driving.

I said to the taxi driver: "King Arthur's Close." He said: "Don't worry, we'll lose him at the next set of lights." – Tommy Cooper

A bus is a vehicle that travels twice as fast when you are running after it as it does when you're on it.

I couldn't get my fridge to work this morning. So I took the bus instead.

***

TRUTHS

No matter how much you push the envelope, it will still be stationary.

Change is inevitable, except from a vending machine.

The shin bone is a device for finding furniture in a dark room.

The severity of the itch is directly proportional to the reach.

A clear conscience is usually the sign of a bad memory.

Some cause happiness wherever they go; others, whenever they go. – Oscar Wilde

The easiest way to find something lost around the house is to buy a replacement.

When everything is coming your way, you're in the wrong lane.

The only substitute for good manners is fast reflexes.

The problem with kleptomaniacs is they always take things literally.

If life gives you melons, you might be dyslexic.

The most effective way to remember your partner's birthday is to forget it once.

Happiness is like peeing in your pants. Everyone can see it, but only you can feel the warmth.

Russian dolls are so full of themselves.

The early bird may get the worm, but it's the second mouse that gets the cheese.

The easiest time to add insult to injury is when you're signing someone's cast. – Demetri Martin

People will believe anything if you whisper it.

One day, you're the best thing since sliced bread. The next, you're toast.

Time may be a great healer, but it's a lousy beautician.

If you think nobody cares about you, try missing a couple of mortgage payments.

A bird in the hand is safer than one overhead.

The only time the world beats a path to your door is when you're in the bathroom.

The nurse who can smile when things go wrong is probably going off duty.

The road to success is always under construction.

Light travels faster than sound, which is why some people appear bright until you hear them speak.

**

TV AND MOVIES

I got offered a great TV, but the volume control is broken and is always on full. It was only £20. I couldn't turn it down.

I saw a documentary on how ships are kept together. Riveting! – Stewart Francis

I'm surprised to see that one TV channel is screening the World Origami Championships. It's on paperview.

TV evening news is where the presenter begins with "good evening" and then proceeds to tell you why it isn't.

The unluckiest guy in US TV cop shows must be Officer Down. He's always getting shot.

The History Channel + 1: where history repeats itself.

I think the Discovery Channel should be on a different channel each day.

Why didn't Lady Penelope ever sleep with any of the *Thunderbirds* pilots? – She knew it would end in a complicated, tangled mess.

Did you watch that TV show about obesity in the navy? It got the biggest ratings.

I used to watch golf on TV, but my doctor said I needed more exercise. So now I watch tennis on TV.

The human race is faced with a cruel choice: work or daytime TV.

Al Pacino is to star in a new movie about a man who wins the World Knitting Championships. It's called *Scarf Ace*.

What Disney film features a lot of swearing and cursing? – *101 Damnations*.

What's ET short for? – He's only got little legs.

Did you hear about the movie *Constipation*? It hasn't come out yet.

Have you heard of that new film about a tractor? I just saw the trailer.

The badness of a movie is directly proportional to the number of helicopters in it.

Did you ever see the French movie *And*? I think it was released in this country as *ET.* – Milton Jones

Our local cinema owner died last night. His funeral is on Wednesday at 2.00, 4.45 and 7.30.

***

WEDDINGS

What do cannibals do at a wedding? – Toast the bride and groom.

My sister had a fairytale wedding. Grimm.

The Invisible Man married an invisible woman. Their kids were nothing to look at. – Tommy Cooper

A limbo dancer married a locksmith. The wedding was low key.

They married for better or worse. He couldn't have done better and she couldn't have done worse.

A Hollywood wedding is one where they take each other for better or worse, but not for long.

Why did the husband like to watch his wedding video backwards? – So he could see himself walking out of the church a free man.

What are the top three occasions that require witnesses? Crimes, accidents and marriages. Need I say more?

What's the difference between a nudist wedding and an ordinary wedding? – At a nudist wedding you don't have to ask who the best man is.

A best man's speech should be like a mini-skirt: short enough to be interesting, but long enough to cover the bare essentials.

Why do married people spin their wedding ring? – They are trying to work out the combination.

The wedding invite said "Simon Feilder plus one". So I turned up an hour late. – Simon Feilder

So apparently RSVPing back to a wedding invite "maybe next time" isn't the correct response.

***

WORK

Employee of the month is a good example of how somebody can be both a winner and a loser at the same time. – Demetri Martin

Teamwork is important. It helps to put the blame on someone else.

Robinson Crusoe pioneered the 40-hour week. He had all the work done by Friday.

Most people are shocked when they find out what a bad electrician I am.

I've found a job helping a one-armed typist do capital letters. It's shift work.

A bus station is where a bus stops. A train station is where a train stops. On my desk I have a workstation.

I didn't like being a coach driver. I was convinced people were talking behind my back.

Cleaning mirrors is a job I could really see myself doing.

Despite removing all the stains, I still lost my job as a church window cleaner.

I can't believe I got fired from the calendar factory. All I did was take a day off.

I just got fired from my job as a set designer. I left without making a scene.

I quit my job at the helium factory. I didn't like being spoken to in that tone of voice. – Stewart Francis

A friend of mine lost his job at a fishing supplies company. He opened a whole can of worms.

I got fired from my job at the funeral parlour. My boss thought "smoking or non-smoking" was an inappropriate way to ask if they wanted cremation.

I just got fired from my job as a taxi driver. It turns out people *don't* like it when you go the extra mile for them.

I gave up my seat to a blind person on the bus. That's how I lost my job as a bus driver.

I always give 100 per cent. Which is why I lost my job as an exam marker.

I don't think I could cope with a job as a coffee taster. How do they sleep at night?

I did have a friend who worked at a coffee shop, but quit because he couldn't stand the daily grind.

I once went for a job as a blacksmith. The guy asked me if I had ever shoed a horse. I said: "No, but I've told a donkey to go away."

When my boss asked me who's the stupid one, me or him, I told him everyone knows he doesn't hire stupid people.

Tarzan came home from a hard day's work and said: "Jane, it's a jungle out there."

My dad said: "Always leave them wanting more." Ironically, that's how he lost his job in disaster relief. – Mark Watson

A tidy desk is a sign of an untidy desk drawer.

My boss says he is going to fire the employee with the worst posture. I have a hunch, it might be me.

Did you hear about the sacked dodgem supervisor who took his former employers to court? He was suing them for funfair dismissal.

I used to be a builder for 158 years, but that's just an estimate.

The worst part about working for the department of unemployment is when you get fired you still have to show up the next day.

He who laughs last at the boss's jokes probably isn't far from retirement.

Sexual harassment at work – is it a problem for the self-employed? – Victoria Wood

It's quite difficult to get a job at Citroën. I had to send them 2 CVs.

When I worked as a driver, I delivered a giant roll of bubble wrap to a customer. He said: "Pop it in the corner." It took me three and a half hours.

As I get older and I remember all the people I've lost along the way, I think to myself, "Maybe a career as a tour guide wasn't for me."